THE LITTLE RED BOOK OF
LOVE

THE LITTLE RED BOOK OF
LOVE

Edited by Kari Belsheim

Skyhorse Publishing

Skyhorse Publishing books may be purchased in bulk at special discounts for sales promotion, corporate gifts, fund-raising, or educational purposes. Special editions can also be created to specifications. For details, contact the Special Sales Department, Skyhorse Publishing, 307 West 36th Street, 11th Floor, New York, NY 10018 or info@skyhorsepublishing.com.

Skyhorse® and Skyhorse Publishing® are registered trademarks of Skyhorse Publishing, Inc.®, a Delaware corporation.

www.skyhorsepublishing.com

10 9 8 7 6 5 4 3 2 1

Library of Congress Cataloging-in-Publication Data is available on file.

ISBN: 978-1-62636-198-0

Printed in China

CONTENTS

Introduction

Because it is so overwhelming, love can be difficult to express. We find that words are insufficient. When we do find the words that hit the mark and reflect those indefinable feelings, it means the world. Maybe we find this in a novel or perhaps in a movie. These moments often take us by surprise, just as love does.

As I curated this collection of words on love, I couldn't help but notice their rich variety. Love is, in many ways, an individual education. We learn how to love from the unique people around us, and hopefully we only get better and better at it.

My earliest lessons on love came from my family. My father would put my brother, sister, and me to bed at night, taking the time to tuck each of us in. I would often ask for a "whisker rub" from his scraggly chin, along with a hug good-night. Even when I was a teenager, my parents would make me breakfast every morning. These are very simple ways to say "I love you," but I've found the smallest gestures to often mean the most.

Whether you wish to celebrate love in its simplicity or reckon with its complex power, I hope you will enjoy this collection of words on love; our driving force, and our saving grace.

—Kari Belsheim,
New York

CHAPTER 1

WHAT IS LOVE?

The real lover is the man who can thrill you by kissing your forehead or smiling into your eyes or just staring into space.
—MARILYN MONROE

• • •

We're all a little weird. And life is a little weird. And when we find someone whose weirdness is compatible with ours, we join up with them and fall into mutually satisfying weirdness—and call it love—true love.
—ROBERT FULGHUM, *True Love*

• • •

Love is an irresistible desire to be irresistibly desired.
—ROBERT FROST

• • •

One word frees us of all the weight and pain of life:
that word is love.
—SOPHOCLES

• • •

Romance is the glamour which turns the dust of
everyday life into a golden haze.
—ELINOR GLYN

• • •

A purpose of human life, no matter who is controlling it,
is to love whoever is around to be loved.
—KURT VONNEGUT, *The Sirens of Titan*

• • •

Love is not love which alters when it alteration finds, or bends
with the remover to remove. O no, it is an ever-fixed mark
that looks on tempest and is never shaken . . .
—WILLIAM SHAKESPEARE, *Great Sonnets*

• • •

The power of a glance has been so much abused in love
stories, that it has come to be disbelieved in. Few people dare
now to say that two beings have fallen in love because they
have looked at each other. Yet it is in this way that love begins,
and in this way only.
—VICTOR HUGO, *Les Misérables*

• • •

"How do you spell 'love'?"
"You don't spell it. . . . You feel it."
—PIGLET AND POOH, A. A. Milne, *Winnie the Pooh*

• • •

If it is true that there are as many minds as there are heads,
then there are as many kinds of love as there are hearts.
—LEO TOLSTOY, *Anna Karenina*

• • •

I have feelings too. I am still human. All I want is to be loved,
for myself and for my talent.
—MARILYN MONROE

• • •

What she had realized was that love was that moment when
your heart was about to burst.
—STIEG LARSSON, *The Girl with the Dragon Tattoo*

• • •

Love is a springtime plant that perfumes everything with its
hope, even the ruins to which it clings.
—GUSTAVE FLAUBERT

• • •

You know you're in love when you can't fall asleep because
reality is finally better than your dreams.
—DR. SEUSS

• • •

I like to believe that love is a reciprocal thing, that it can't
really be felt, truly, by one.
—SEAN PENN

• • •

Love is composed of a single soul inhabiting two bodies.
—ARISTOTLE

• • •

Love, to me, is someone telling me, "I want to be with you for
the rest of my life, and if you needed me to, I'd jump out of a
plane for you."
—JENNIFER LOPEZ

• • •

You know it's love when all you want is that person to be
happy, even if you're not part of their happiness.
—JULIA ROBERTS

• • •

Love is absolute loyalty. People fade, looks fade,
but loyalty never fades. You can depend so much on
certain people; you can set your watch by them. And that's
love, even if it doesn't seem very exciting.
—SYLVESTER STALLONE

• • •

A loving heart is the beginning of all knowledge.
—THOMAS CARLYLE

• • •

Love is an emotion experienced by the many and
enjoyed by the few.
—GEORGE JEAN NATHAN

• • •

Love is a force more formidable than any other. It is invisible—it cannot be seen or measured, yet powerful enough to transform you in a moment, and offer you more joy than any material possession could.
—BARBARA DE ANGELIS

• • •

Love is life. And if you miss love, you miss life.
—LEO BUSCAGLIA

• • •

Love is not a mere impulse, it must contain truth, which is law.
—RABINDRANATH TAGORE

• • •

Love is a game that two can play and both win.
—EVA GABOR

• • •

True love is like ghosts, which everybody talks about and
few have seen.
—FRANÇOIS DE LA ROCHEFOUCAULD

• • •

Love is a friendship set to music.
—JOSEPH CAMPBELL

• • •

Love is the triumph of imagination over intelligence.
—H. L. MENCKEN

• • •

To love another person is to see the face of God.
—VICTOR HUGO, *Les Misérables*

• • •

It's an unexplainable feeling, an expression. It's a touch,
it's a feel. Once you feel it, it's like no other thing in the world.
—SNOOP DOGG

• • •

Art and love are the same thing. It's the process of seeing
yourself in things that are not you.
—CHUCK KLOSTERMAN, *Killing Yourself to Live*

• • •

Love is the idler's occupation, the warrior's relaxation,
and the sovereign's ruination.
—NAPOLEON BONAPARTE

• • •

Love is a canvas furnished by nature and embroidered
by imagination.
—VOLTAIRE

• • •

Love is a gross exaggeration of the difference between
one person and everybody else.
—GEORGE BERNARD SHAW

• • •

Love is being stupid together.
—PAUL VALÉRY

• • •

Love is the only sane and satisfactory answer to the problem of human existence.
—ERICH FROMM

• • •

Love is the greatest refreshment in life.
—PABLO PICASSO

• • •

Love is everything it's cracked up to be. . . . It really is worth fighting for, being brave for, risking everything for.
—ERICA JONG

• • •

We love because it's the only true adventure.
—NIKKI GIOVANNI

• • •

Love is a taste of paradise.
—SHOLEM ALEICHEM

• • •

I believe love is primarily a choice and only
sometimes a feeling. If you want to feel love, choose to
love and be patient.
—REAL LIVE PREACHER

• • •

You know it's love when you want to keep holding hands
even after you're sweaty.
—ANONYMOUS

• • •

I was nauseous and tingly all over. I was either in love or
I had smallpox.
—WOODY ALLEN

• • •

Love is a flower that grows in any soil, works its sweet
miracles undaunted by autumn frost or winter snow,
blooming fair and fragrant all the year, and blessing those
who give and those who receive.
—LOUISA MAY ALCOTT, *Little Men*

• • •

Love is a seeking for a way of life; the way that cannot be
followed alone; the resonance of all spiritual and
physical things.
—ANSEL ADAMS, *Letter to Cedric Wright*

• • •

There are several kinds of love. One is a selfish, mean,
grasping, egotistical thing which uses love for
self-importance. This is the ugly and crippling kind.
The other is an outpouring of everything good in you—of
kindness and consideration and respect—not only the
social respect of manners but the greater respect which is
recognition of another person as unique and valuable.
—JOHN STEINBECK, *Steinbeck: A Life in Letters*

• • •

Love is what you make it. Unfortunately, I can't make it today,
as I have a doctor's appointment.
—JAROD KINTZ, *This Book is Not For Sale*

• • •

Love is the source of reality.
—SUSAN POLIS SCHUTZ

• • •

Love is how you stay alive, even after you are gone.
—MITCH ALBOM, *Tuesdays with Morrie*

• • •

Love isn't a state of perfect caring. It is an active noun like struggle. To love someone is to strive to accept that person exactly the way he or she is, right here and now.
—FRED ROGERS, *The World According to Mister Rogers: Important Things to Remember*

• • •

Love is needing someone. Love is putting up with someone's bad qualities because they somehow complete you.
—SARAH DESSEN, *This Lullaby*

• • •

True love is not so much a matter of romance as it
is a matter of anxious concern for the well-being of
one's companion.
—GORDON B. HINCKLEY, *Stand a Little Taller*

• • •

Love is not affectionate feeling, but a steady wish for the
loved person's ultimate good as it can be obtained.
—C. S. LEWIS

• • •

Sometimes it's a form of love just to talk to somebody
that you have nothing in common with and still be
fascinated by their presence.
—DAVID BYRNE

• • •

Love means never having to say you're sorry.
—OLIVER BARRETT IV (RYAN O'NEAL), *Love Story*

• • •

Love is something sent from Heaven to worry the
Hell out of you.
—DOLLY PARTON

• • •

I think love is another way to create, as cheesy as
that sounds.
—CHANNING TATUM

• • •

Without being corny, we try simply to be considerate to each other every day rather than lavishing each other with gifts.
—HELEN MIRREN

• • •

One of the best feelings in the world is knowing that your presence and absence both mean something to someone.
—ANONYMOUS

• • •

My parents danced together, her head on his chest. Both had their eyes closed. They seemed so perfectly content. If you can find someone like that, someone who you can hold and close your eyes to the world with, then you're lucky. Even if it only lasts for a minute or a day.
—PATRICK ROTHFUSS, *The Name of the Wind*

• • •

Love can turn a man into a beast. But love can also make an ugly man handsome.
—THE BEAST (JEAN MARAIS), *Beauty and the Beast*

• • •

To make the journey and not fall deeply in love, well, you haven't lived a life at all.
—WILLIAM PARRISH (ANTHONY HOPKINS),
Meet Joe Black

• • •

There are too many mediocre things in life to deal with and love shouldn't be one of them.
—DAVID SCHRADER (MACKENZIE ASTIN),
Dream for an Insomniac

• • •

When love feels like magic, you call it destiny. When destiny has a sense of humor, you call it serendipity.
—*SERENDIPITY*

• • •

CHAPTER 2

AGONY

We accept the love we think we deserve.
—STEPHEN CHBOSKY, *The Perks of Being a Wallflower*

• • •

Have you ever been in love? Horrible isn't it? It makes you so
vulnerable. It opens your chest and it opens up your heart and
it means that someone can get inside you and mess you up.
—NEIL GAIMAN, *The Sandman Chronicles, Vol. 9: The
Kindly Ones*

• • •

I am two fools, I know, for loving, and for saying so
in whining poetry.
—JOHN DONNE

• • •

Love is like a nettle that stings badly.
—RUSSIAN PROVERB

• • •

Love never dies a natural death.
—ANAÏS NIN

• • •

They do not love that do not show their love. The course of
true love never did run smooth. Love is a familiar.
Love is a devil. There is no evil angel but Love.
—WILLIAM SHAKESPEARE, *Love's Labours Lost*

• • •

Just when you think it can't get any worse, it can. And just
when you think it can't get any better, it can.
—NICHOLAS SPARKS, *At First Sight*

• • •

The one you love and the one who loves you are never,
ever the same person.
—CHUCK PALAHNIUK, *Invisible Monsters*

• • •

Love is a fire. But whether it is going to warm your hearth or
burn down your house, you never can tell.
—JOAN CRAWFORD

• • •

Some women choose to follow men, and some women choose to follow their dreams. If you're wondering which way to go, remember that your career will never wake up and tell you that it doesn't love you anymore.
—LADY GAGA

• • •

The heart was made to be broken.
—OSCAR WILDE

• • •

You can suffer without love, but you can't love without suffering.
—GERMAN PROVERB

• • •

Love does not begin and end the way we seem to think it does.
Love is a battle, love is a war; love is a growing up.
—JAMES BALDWIN

• • •

The only thing worse than a boy who hates you:
a boy that loves you.
—MARKUS ZUSAK, *The Book Thief*

• • •

You pierce my soul. I am half agony, half hope. . . .
I have loved non but you.
—JANE AUSTEN, *Persuasion*

• • •

I crave your mouth, your voice, your hair. Silent and starving,
I prowl through the streets. Bread does not nourish me,
dawn disrupts me, all day I hunt for the liquid measure of
your steps.
—PABLO NERUDA

• • •

I would die for you. But I won't live for you.
—STEPHEN CHBOSKY, *The Perks of Being a Wallflower*

• • •

Declarations of love amuse me. Especially when unrequited.
—CASSANDRA CLARE, *City of Bones*

• • •

If you gave someone your heart and they died, did they take it with them? Did you spend the rest of forever with a hold inside you that couldn't be filled?
—JODI PICOULT, *Nineteen Minutes*

• • •

Be careful of love. It'll twist your brain around and leave you thinking up is down and right is wrong.
—RICK RIORDAN, *The Battle of the Labyrinth*

• • •

First love is like a snake; if it doesn't destroy you, it will paralyze you.
—POLISH PROVERB

• • •

Love is so short, forgetting is so long.
—PAULO COELHO

• • •

There are a thousand miseries in one love.
—INDIAN PROVERB

• • •

What is Love? I have met in the streets a very poor young
man who was in love. His hat was old, his coat worn,
the water passed through his shoes and the stars through
his soul.
—VICTOR HUGO

• • •

It takes courage to love, but pain through love is the
purifying fire which those who love generously know.
We all know people who are so much afraid of pain that
they shut themselves up like clams in a shell and, giving out
nothing, receive nothing and therefore shrink until life is
a mere living death.
—ELEANOR ROOSEVELT

• • •

He that marries for love, dies miserably of anger.
—ITALIAN PROVERB

• • •

If all else perished, and he remained, I should continue to be;
and if all else remained, and he were annihilated,
the universe would turn to a mighty stranger.
—EMILY BRONTË, *Wuthering Heights*

• • •

Sometimes love means letting go when you want to hold
on tighter.
—MELISSA MARR, *Ink Exchange*

● ● ●

Never love anyone who treats you like you're ordinary.
—OSCAR WILDE

● ● ●

You know how they say you only hurt the ones you love? Well,
it works both ways.
—CHUCK PALAHNIUK, *Fight Club*

● ● ●

Love is an untamed force. When we try to control it,
it destroys us. When we try to imprison it, it enslaves us.
When we try to understand it, it leaves us feeling lost
and confused.
—PAULO COELHO

• • •

This hole in my heart is in the shape of you and no-one else
can fit it. Why would I want them to?
—JEANETTE WINTERSON, *Written on the Body*

• • •

There are only two tragedies in life: one is not getting what
one wants, and the other is getting it.
—OSCAR WILDE

• • •

Yield to the desires of your body, then endure the
disasters that follow.
—RUSSIAN PROVERB

• • •

Love sucks. Sometimes it feels good. Sometimes it's just
another way to bleed.
—LAURELL K. HAMILTON, *Blue Moon*

• • •

I wish I had died before I ever loved anyone but her.
—ERNEST HEMINGWAY, *A Moveable Feast*

• • •

I'm not sentimental—I'm **as** romantic as you are.
The idea, you know, is that the sentimental person thinks
things will last—the romantic person has a desperate
confidence that they won't.
—F. SCOTT FITZGERALD, *This Side of Paradise*

• • •

Nothing takes the taste out of peanut butter quite like
unrequited love.
—CHARLES M. SCHULZ, "Peanuts"

• • •

The voice of Love seemed to call to me, but it was a
wrong number.
—P. G. WODEHOUSE, *Very Good, Jeeves!*

• • •

Yet each man kills the thing he loves . . .
—OSCAR WILDE, "The Ballad of Reading Gaol"

• • •

In secret we met—
In silence I grieve,
That thy heart could forget,
Thy spirit deceive.
—GEORGE GORDON BYRON, "When We Two Parted"

• • •

Ever has it been that love knows not its own depth
until the hour of separation.
—KAHLIL GIBRAN

• • •

To love is to suffer. To avoid suffering, one must not love. But then, one suffers from loving. Therefore, to love is to suffer; not to love is to suffer; to suffer is to suffer. To be happy is to love. To be happy, then is to suffer, but suffering makes one unhappy. Therefore, to be happy, one must love or love to suffer or suffer from too much happiness.
—WOODY ALLEN

• • •

The prayers of a lover are more imperious than the menaces of the whole world.
—GEORGE SAND

• • •

You know, what can I say? If a relationship can't work out, make a record.
—MILEY CYRUS

• • •

Hearts will never be practical until they are made unbreakable.
—THE WIZARD OF OZ (FRANK MORGAN),
The Wizard of Oz

• • •

Lovers who love truly do not write down their happiness.
—ANATOLE FRANCE, *The Crime of Sylvestre Bonnard*

• • •

He promised her that he would give her everything, everything she wanted, as men in love always do. And she trusted him despite herself, as women in love always do.
—PHILIPPA GREGORY, *The White Queen*

• • •

"Is that love, do you think?" he asks, sounding genuinely curious. "Being crazy about someone no matter how much they hurt you?"
—STACEY JAY, *Juliet Immortal*

• • •

Even when a river of tears courses through this body, the flame of love cannot be quenched.
—IZUMI SHIKIBU

• • •

Love is a kind of warfare.
—OVID

• • •

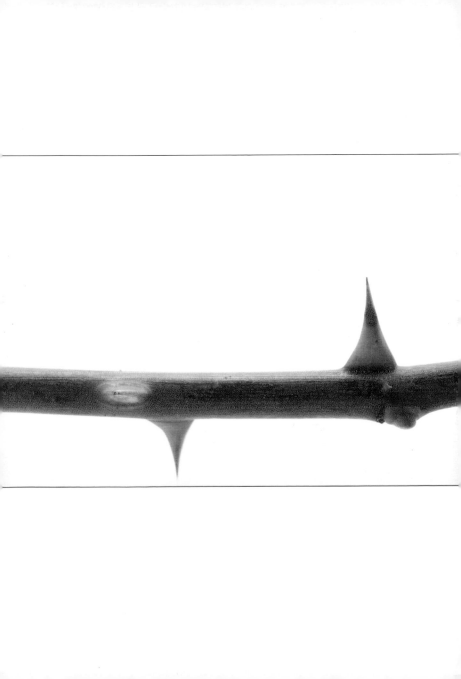

Only time can heal your broken heart, just as only time can
heal his broken arms and legs.
—MISS PIGGY, *Miss Piggy's Guide to Life*

• • •

Don't settle for a relationship that won't let you be yourself.
—OPRAH WINFREY

• • •

Pleasure of love lasts but a moment. Pain of love lasts a
lifetime.
—BETTE DAVIS

• • •

Men are a luxury. Not a necessity.
—CHER

• • •

If you can love someone with your whole heart, even one person, then there's salvation in life. Even if you can't get together with that person.
—HARUKI MURAKAMI, *1Q84*

• • •

It is well for the heart to be naïve and the mind not to be.
—ANATOLE FRANCE

• • •

Life is messy . . . love is messier.
—*CATCH AND RELEASE*

• • •

I'm scared of walking out of this room and never feeling the
rest of my whole life the way I feel when I'm with you.
—FRANCES "BABY" HOUSEMAN (JENNIFER GREY),
Dirty Dancing

• • •

When you break up, your whole identity is shattered.
It's like death.
—DENNIS QUAID

• • •

The best way to mend a broken heart is time and girlfriends.
—GWYNETH PALTROW

• • •

A wise girl kisses but doesn't love, listens but doesn't believe,
and leaves before she is left.
—MARILYN MONROE

• • •

As long as you know most men are like children, you
know everything.
—COCO CHANEL

• • •

The greater your capacity to love, the greater your capacity
to feel the pain.
—JENNIFER ANISTON

• • •

Men should be like Kleenex: soft, strong, disposable.
—CHER

• • •

Love is like a rose. It looks beautiful on the outside . . .
but there is always pain hidden somewhere.
—ANATOLE FRANCE

• • •

If you live to be a hundred, I want to live to be a hundred minus one day so I never have to live without you.
—A. A. MILNE, *The House at Pooh Corner*

• • •

Friendship always benefits; love sometimes injures.
—SENECA

• • •

Friendship often ends in love; but love in friendship, never.
—CHARLES CALEB COLTON

• • •

In love, unlike most other passions, the recollection of what you have had and lost is always better than what you can hope for in the future.
—STENDHAL, *De L'Amour*

• • •

Love can sometimes be magic. But magic can sometimes . . . just be an illusion.
—JAVAN

• • •

The way to love anything is to realize that it may be lost.
—GILBERT K. CHESTERTON

• • •

A woman's heart is a deep ocean of secrets.
—ROSE DAWSON (GLORIA STUART), *Titanic*

• • •

When you end up happily married, even the failed
relationships have worked beautifully to get you there.
—JULIA ROBERTS

• • •

Oh, love isn't there to make us happy. I believe it exists to
show us how much we can endure.
—HERMANN HESSE, *Peter Camenzind*

• • •

Angry, and half in love with her, and tremendously sorry,
I turned away.
—F. SCOTT FITZGERALD, *The Great Gatsby*

• • •

Love is a trap. When it appears, we see only its light,
not its shadows.
—PAULO COELHO

• • •

Love is an exploding cigar we willingly smoke.
—LYNDA BARRY

• • •

There's definitely a dangerous feeling when you're in love. . . .
It's giving your heart to someone else and knowing that they
have control over your feelings. I know for me, who always
tries to be so tough, that's the dangerous thing.
—BEYONCÉ KNOWLES

• • •

God save me from my friends—I can protect myself from
my enemies.
—PROVERB

• • •

Men kick friendship around like a football, but it doesn't
seem to crack. Women treat it like glass, and it goes to pieces.
—ANNE MORROW LINDBERGH

• • •

Once you have loved someone, you'd do anything in the
world for them . . . except love them again.
—ANONYMOUS

• • •

Be with me always. Take any form, drive me mad, only do not
leave me in this dark alone where I cannot find you.
I cannot live without my life! I cannot die without my soul.
—HEATHCLIFF (LAURENCE OLIVIER), *Wuthering
Heights*

• • •

To hell with God damned "L'Amour." It always causes far more
trouble than it is worth. Don't run after it. Don't court it. Keep
it waiting off stage until you're good and ready for it and even
then treat it with the suspicious disdain that it deserves. . . .
—NOËL COWARD, *Letter to Marlene Dietrich*

• • •

He does something to me, that boy. Every time. It's his only
detriment. He steps on my heart. He makes me cry.
—MARKUS ZUSAK, *The Book Thief*

• • •

Last time I saw you, I said that it hurt too much to love you.
But I was wrong about that. The truth is it hurts too much not
to love you.
—P. C. CAST

• • •

I wonder how many people don't get the one they want, but
end up with the one they're supposed to be with.
—FANNIE FLAGG, *Fried Green Tomatoes at the
Whistle Stop Café*

• • •

If in loving them we do not love what they are, but only their
potential likeness to ourselves, then we do not love them: we
only love the reflection of ourselves we find in them.
—THOMAS MERTON, *No Man Is an Island*

• • •

Let our scars fall in love.
—GALWAY KINNELL

• • •

Love can consign us to hell or to paradise, but it always takes
us somewhere.
—PAULO COELHO, *By the River Piedra I Sat Down
and Wept*

• • •

Don't cry over someone who wouldn't cry over you.
—LAUREN CONRAD

• • •

Let me die the moment my love dies. Let me not outlive
my own capacity to love. Let me die still loving, and so,
never die.
—MARY ZIMMERMAN, *Metamorphoses*

• • •

If you love something set it free, but don't be surprised if it
comes back with herpes.
—CHUCK PALAHNIUK

• • •

Welcome to the wonderful world of jealousy, he thought.
For the price of admission, you get a splitting headache, a
nearly irresistible urge to commit murder, and an inferiority
complex. Yippee.
—J. R. WARD, *Dark Lover*

• • •

The truth is, everyone is going to hurt you. You just got to find the ones worth suffering for.
—BOB MARLEY

● ● ●

It isn't possible to love and part. You will wish that it was. You can transmute love, ignore it, muddle it, but you can never pull it out of you. I know by experience that the poets are right: love is eternal.
—E. M. FORSTER, *A Room with a View*

● ● ●

If I can stop one heart from breaking, I shall not live in vain.
—EMILY DICKINSON

● ● ●

You have to love. You have to feel. It is the reason you are here on earth. You are here to risk your heart. You are here to be swallowed up. And when it happens that you are broken, or betrayed, or left, or hurt, or death brushes near, let yourself sit by an apple tree and listen to the apples falling all around you in heaps, wasting their sweetness. Tell yourself you tasted as many as you could.
—LOUISE ERDRICH, *The Painted Drum*

• • •

Tell me you love me. Tell me, because if I tell you first, I'm afraid you'll think it's a game. Save me . . . I beg of you.
—SOPHIE KOWALSKI (MARION COTILLARD), *Love Me If You Dare*

• • •

Men like to squash you. I just want someone who's happy with himself, happy with his life. He doesn't have to squash mine.
—SARAH SILVERMAN

• • •

One of the hardest things in life is having words in your heart that you can't utter.
—JAMES EARL JONES

• • •

I'm so mad at you. I'm really mad at you for what you did. But I'm mad at myself too. Because I should not have jumped out of that car—I should have fought for you. Because you fight for your soul mates.
—CAL WEAVER (STEVE CARELL), *Crazy, Stupid, Love.*

• • •

Love is the hardest habit to break, and the most difficult to satisfy.
—DREW BARRYMORE

• • •

If you want to read about love and marriage, you've got to buy two separate books.
—ALAN KING

• • •

Do you know that place between asleep and awake? That place where you still remember dreaming? That's where I'll always love you, Peter Pan. That's where I'll be waiting.
—TINKERBELL (JULIA ROBERTS), *Hook*

• • •

Most people have a harder time letting themselves love than finding someone to love them.
—BILL RUSSELL

• • •

True friends cry when you leave. Fake friends leave
when you cry.
—ANONYMOUS

• • •

Animals are such agreeable friends—they ask no questions,
they pass no criticisms.
—GEORGE ELIOT, *Mr. Gilfil's Love Story*

• • •

When something or someone is no longer bringing you up,
but pulling you down—it's time to let go. When something
or someone is no longer adding to your life, but subtracting
from it—it's time to go.
—MANDY HALE, *The Single Woman's Sassy Survival Guide:
Letting Go and Moving On*

• • •

Those whom we most love are often the most alien to us.
—CHRISTOPHER PAOLINI, *Eldest*

• • •

You cannot say no to the people you love, not often.
That's the secret. And then when you do, it has to sound like a
yes. Or you have to make them say no. You have to take time
and trouble.
—MARIO PUZO, *The Godfather*

• • •

You can't help whom you love, Lady. Nor can you know
what it's liable to cause you to do.
—KRISTIN CASHORE, *Fire*

• • •

Don't wait for someone else to complete you.
Jerry Maguire was just a movie.
—OPRAH WINFREY

• • •

As my mom has said, when one person is unhappy,
it usually means two people are unhappy but that one has
not come to terms with it yet.
—MINDY KALING, *Is Everyone Hanging Out Without Me?*

• • •

I mean, I love being with friends and I love kissing and loving
someone to pieces. But it's hard to find someone who doesn't
ultimately start judging you and your choices.
—SARAH SILVERMAN

• • •

Tis better to have loved and lost than never to have loved
at all.
—ALFRED TENNYSON, *In Memoriam*

• • •

This is a good sign, having a broken heart. It means we have
tried for something.
—ELIZABETH GILBERT, *Eat, Pray, Love*

• • •

And then you shot across my sky like a meteor. Suddenly
everything was on fire; there was brilliancy, there was beauty.
When you were gone, when the meteor had fallen over the
horizon, everything went black. Nothing had changed, but
my eyes were blinded by the light. I couldn't see the stars
anymore. And there was no more reason, for anything.
—STEPHENIE MEYER, *New Moon*

• • •

CHAPTER 3

PASSION

For God's sake hold your tongue, and let me love.
—JOHN DONNE

• • •

Dumbledore watched her fly away, and as her silvery glow
faded he turned back to Snape, and his eyes were full of tears.
"After all this time?" "Always," said Snape.
—J. K. ROWLING, *Harry Potter and the Deathly Hallows*

• • •

Two people in love, alone, isolated from the world,
that's beautiful.
—MILAN KUNDERA

• • •

Nobody has ever measured, not even poets, how much the
heart can hold.
—ZELDA FITZGERALD

• • •

Any man who can drive safely while kissing a pretty girl is
simply not giving the kiss the attention it deserves.
—ALBERT EINSTEIN

• • •

What I want is to be needed. What I need is to be indispensable to somebody. Who I need is somebody that will eat up all my free time, my ego, my attention. Somebody addicted to me. A mutual addiction.
—CHUCK PALAHNIUK, *Choke*

• • •

I love you as certain dark things are to be loved, in secret, between the shadow and the soul.
—PABLO NERUDA

• • •

Doubt thou the stars are fire; doubt that the sun doth move; doubt truth to be a liar; but never doubt I love.
—WILLIAM SHAKESPEARE, *Hamlet*

• • •

I read once that the ancient Egyptians had fifty words for sand and the Eskimos had a hundred words for snow. I wish I had a thousand words for love, but all that comes to mind is the way you move against me while you sleep and there are no words for that.
—BRIAN ANDREAS, *Story People: Selected Stories and Drawings of Brian Andreas*

• • •

When I saw you I fell in love, and you smiled because you knew.
—ARRIGO BOITO

• • •

I loved you like a man loves a woman he never touches, only writes to, keeps little photographs of.
—CHARLES BUKOWSKI, *Love Is a Dog from Hell*

• • •

It was a million tiny little things that, when you added them all up, they meant we were supposed to be together . . . and I knew it.
—SAM BALDWIN (TOM HANKS), *Sleepless in Seattle*

• • •

I believe in love because I had it for so long, so I know it's possible.
—ZOE SALDANA

• • •

Don't forget I'm just a girl, standing in front of a boy, asking him to love her.
—ANNA (JULIA ROBERTS), *Notting Hill*

• • •

The simple thing of just having somebody to lay your head on.
Oh, it makes me want to cry right now.
—BRITNEY SPEARS

• • •

Listen to me, mister. You're my knight in shining armor.
Don't forget it.
—ETHEL (KATHARINE HEPBURN), *On Golden Pond*

• • •

We loved with a love that was more than love.
—EDGAR ALLEN POE, "Annabel Lee"

• • •

There is always some madness in love. But there is also always some reason in madness.
—FRIEDRICH NIETZSCHE

• • •

I love you also means I love you more than anyone loves you, or has loved you, or will love you, and also, I love you in a way that no one loves you, or has loved you, or will love you, and also, I love you in a way that I love no one else, and never have loved anyone else, and never will love anyone else.
—JONATHAN SAFRAN FOER

• • •

I love you, and I will love you until I die, and if there is life after that, I'll love you then.
—CASSANDRA CLARE, *City of Glass*

• • •

Gravitation is not responsible for people falling in love.
—ALBERT EINSTEIN

• • •

Of all forms of caution, caution in love is perhaps the most
fatal to true happiness.
—BERTRAND RUSSELL, *The Conquest of Happiness*

• • •

He's more myself than I am. Whatever our souls are made of,
his and mine are the same.
—EMILY BRONTË, *Wuthering Heights*

• • •

Promise me you'll never forget me because if I thought you
would, I'd never leave.
—A. A. MILNE, *Winnie the Pooh*

• • •

The heart has its reasons which reason knows not.
—BLAISE PASCAL

• • •

Love has nothing to do with what you are expecting to
get—only with what you are expecting to give—which
is everything.
—KATHARINE HEPBURN, *Me: Stories of My Life*

• • •

I want to do with you what spring does with the cherry trees.
—PABLO NERUDA, *Twenty Love Poems and a Song of Despair*

• • •

Lovers alone wear sunlight.
—E. E. CUMMINGS

• • •

When I am with you, we stay up all night. When you're not here, I can't go to sleep. Praise God for those two insomnias! And the difference between them.
—RUMI

• • •

For it was not into my ear you whispered, but into my heart.
It was not my lips you kissed, but my soul.
—JUDY GARLAND, "My Love Is Lost"

• • •

His heart danced upon her movements like a cork upon a tide.
He heard what her eyes said to him from beneath their cowl
and knew that in some dim past, whether in life or revery, he
had heard their tale before.
—JAMES JOYCE, *A Portrait of the Artist as a Young Man*

• • •

You are like nobody since I love you.
—PABLO NERUDA

• • •

When you have seen as much of life as I have you will not underestimate the power of obsessive love.
—J. K. ROWLING, *Harry Potter and the Half-Blood Prince*

• • •

Kissing—and I mean like, yummy, smacking kissing—is the most delicious, most beautiful and passionate thing that two people can do, bar none. Better than sex, hands down.
—DREW BARRYMORE

• • •

I came here tonight because when you realize you want to spend the rest of your life with a person, you want the rest of your life to start as soon as possible.
—HARRY BURNS (BILLY CRYSTAL), *When Harry Met Sally*

• • •

We are nothing, and we are everything. Look up—every star another world, but what I seek, near or far is love's outline on your face.
—JEANETTE WINTERSON, *The Stone Gods*

• • •

No, I don't think I will kiss you, although you need kissing, badly. That's what's wrong with you. You should be kissed and often, and by someone who knows how.
—RHETT BUTLER (CLARK GABLE), *Gone with the Wind*

• • •

Your heart is free. Have the courage to follow it.
—MALCOLM WALLACE (SEAN LAWLOR), *Braveheart*

• • •

The heart wants what it wants. There's no logic to these things. You meet someone and you fall in love and that's that.
—WOODY ALLEN

• • •

A woman knows the face of the man she loves as a sailor knows the open sea.
—HONORÉ DE BALZAC

• • •

I was born with an enormous need for affection and a terrible need to give it.
—AUDREY HEPBURN

• • •

Time is too slow for those who wait, too swift for those who
fear, too long for those who grieve, too short for those who
rejoice, but for those who love, time is eternity.
—HENRY VAN DYKE

• • •

Absence diminishes mediocre passions and increases great
ones, as the wind extinguishes candles and fans fires.
—FRANÇOIS DE LA ROCHEFOUCAULD

• • •

Love is like war: easy to begin but very hard to stop.
—H. L. MENCKEN

• • •

Come live in my heart and pay no rent.
—SAMUEL LOVER

• • •

If you press me to say why I loved him, I can say no more than
because he was he, and I was I.
—MICHEL DE MONTAIGNE

• • •

Who ever loved that loved not at first sight?
—WILLIAM SHAKESPEARE, *As You Like It*

• • •

I can live without money, but I cannot live without love.
—JUDY GARLAND

• • •

You and you alone make me feel that I am alive. Other men
it is said have seen angels, but I have seen thee and thou art
enough.
—GEORGE EDWARD MOORE, *Letter to Lady Emerald
Cunard*

• • •

I'd rather die tomorrow than live a hundred years without knowing you.
—JOHN SMITH (MEL GIBSON), *Pocahontas*

• • •

To have been loved so deeply, even though the person who loved us is gone, will give us some protection forever.
—J. K. ROWLING, *Harry Potter and the Sorcerer's Stone*

• • •

I would rather spend one lifetime with you than face all the ages of this world alone.
—ARWEN (LIV TYLER), *The Lord of the Rings: The Fellowship of the Ring*

• • •

You're the only boy who makes my heart beat faster and
slower at the same time.
—JESSICA SPENCER (RACHEL McADAMS),
The Hot Chick

• • •

I was about half in love with her by the time we sat down.
That's the thing about girls. Every time they do something
pretty, even if they're not much to look at, or even if they're
sort of stupid, you fall half in love with them, and then you
never know where the hell you are.
—J. D. SALINGER, *The Catcher in the Rye*

• • •

This is it. Life will never be better or sweeter than this.
—NELSON (KEANU REEVES), *Sweet November*

• • •

But for now, let me say—without hope or agenda, just because it's Christmas and at Christmas you tell the truth—to me, you are perfect. And my wasted heart will love you until you look like this [picture of mummy]. Merry Christmas.
—MARK (ANDREW LINCOLN), *Love Actually*

• • •

It's useless to hold a person to anything he says while he's in love, drunk, or running for office.
—SHIRLEY MacLAINE

• • •

He doesn't love you. But I love you. I want you to have your own thoughts and ideas and feelings, even when I hold you in my arms. It's our last chance.
—GEORGE EMERSON (JULIAN SANDS), *A Room with a View*

• • •

I was, and am, swept away. I believe there are some things in life you can't deny or rationalize, and this is one of them.
—CATE BLANCHETT

• • •

You have bewitched me, body and soul, and I love . . .
I love . . . I love you. And I never wish to be parted from you from this day on.
—MR. DARCY (MATTHEW MACFAYDEN),
Pride & Prejudice

• • •

As for me, to love you alone, to make you happy, to do nothing which would contradict your wishes, this is my destiny and the meaning of my life.
—NAPOLEON BONAPARTE

• • •

What I really want to do with my life—what I want to do for a
living—is I want to be with your daughter. I'm good at it.
—LLOYD (JOHN CUSACK), *Say Anything*

• • •

When love is not madness, it is not love.
—PEDRO CALDERÓN DE LA BARCA

• • •

I believe in love and lust and sex and romance. I don't want
everything to add up to some perfect equation. I want mess
and chaos. I want someone to go crazy out of his mind for me.
I want to feel passion and heat and sweat and madness. I want
Valentines and Cupids and all the rest of that crap. I want it all.
—ROSE MORGAN (BARBRA STREISAND), *The Mirror
Has Two Faces*

• • •

Lovers don't finally meet somewhere. They're in each
other all along.
—RUMI

• • •

We are most alive when we're in love.
—JOHN UPDIKE

• • •

I have found that to love and be loved is the most empowering
and exhilarating of all human emotions.
—JANE GOODALL

• • •

If I hadn't met you, I wouldn't like you. If I didn't like you,
I wouldn't love you. If I didn't love you, I wouldn't miss you.
But I did, I do, and I will.
—ANONYMOUS

• • •

Love leads people to become lost in their own feelings and
ignore the world, so it's no surprise their love for the world
goes unrequited.
—BAUVARD, *Evergreens Are Prudish*

• • •

What I want to say is I owe all the happiness of my life to you.
You have been entirely patient with me and incredibly good.
I want to say that—everybody knows it. If anybody could have
saved me it would have been you. Everything has gone from
me but the certainty of your goodness.
—VIRGINIA WOOLF, *Letter to Leonard Woolf*

• • •

All I care about—honest to God—is that you are happy and I don't much care who you'll find happiness with. I mean as long as he's a friendly bloke and treats you nice and kind. If he doesn't I'll come at him with a hammer and clinker. God's eye may be on the sparrow, but my eye will always be on you.
—RICHARD BURTON, *Letter to Elizabeth Taylor*

• • •

Here I am back and still smouldering with passion, like wine smoking. Not a passion any longer for flesh, but a complete hunger for you, a devouring hunger.
—HENRY MILLER, *Letter to Anaïs Nin*

• • •

I dreamed—and this dream was the finest—that all I dreamed was real and true, and we would live in joy forever, you in me, and me in you.
—CLIVE BARKER, *Days of Magic, Nights of War*

• • •

He made me love him without looking at me.
—CHARLOTTE BRONTË, *Jane Eyre*

• • •

I want morning and noon and nightfall with you. I want your tears, your smiles, your kisses . . . the smell of your hair, the taste of your skin, the touch of your breath on my face. I want to see you in the final hour of my life . . . to lie in your arms as I take my last breath.
—LISA KLEYPAS, *Again the Magic*

• • •

I would like to be the air that inhabits you for a moment only. I would like to be that unnoticed and that necessary.
—MARGARET ATWOOD

• • •

You dance inside my chest where no one sees you, but
sometimes I do, and that sight becomes this art.
—RUMI

• • •

I will give you the sun and the rain, and if they are not
available, I will give you a sun check and a rain check. I will
give you all this and more, until I get so exhausted and
depleted that the only way I can recover my energy is by
becoming infatuated with someone else.
—ELIZABETH GILBERT, *Eat, Pray, Love*

• • •

Do I love you? My God, if your love were a grain of sand,
mine would be a universe of beaches.
—WILLIAM GOLDMAN, *The Princess Bride*

• • •

"Maybe . . . you'll fall in love with me all over again."
"Hell," I said, "I love you enough now. What do you want to
do? Ruin me?" "Yes. I want to ruin you." "Good," I said.
"That's what I want too."
—ERNEST HEMINGWAY, *A Farewell to Arms*

• • •

It's dark now and I am very tired. I love you, always.
Time is nothing.
—AUDREY NIFFENEGGER, *The Time Traveler's Wife*

• • •

You are the one girl that made me risk everything for a future
worth having.
—SIMONE ELKELES, *Perfect Chemistry*

• • •

Being with you never felt wrong. It's the one thing I did right.
You're the one thing I did right.
—BECCA FITZPATRICK, *Crescendo*

• • •

I cannot fix on the hour, or the spot, or the look or the words,
which laid the foundation. It is too long ago. I was in the
middle before I knew that I had begun.
—JANE AUSTEN, *Pride and Prejudice*

• • •

My wish is that you may be loved to the point of madness.
—ANDRÉ BRETON, *What Is Surrealism?: Selected Writings*

• • •

Have you ever met a woman who inspires you to love?
Until your every sense is filled with her? You inhale her.
You taste her. You see your unborn child in her eyes and know
that your heart has at last found a home. Your life begins with
her, and without her it must surely end.
—DON JUAN (JOHNNY DEPP), *Don Juan DeMarco*

• • •

Every relationship I've been in, I've overwhelmed the girl.
They just can't handle all the love!
—JUSTIN TIMBERLAKE

• • •

It seems right now that all I've ever done in my life is
making my way here to you.
—ROBERT KINCAID (CLINT EASTWOOD),
The Bridges of Madison County

• • •

If I could ask God one thing, it would be to stop the moon.
Stop the moon and make this night and your beauty
last forever.
—WILLIAM THATCHER (HEATH LEDGER),
A Knight's Tale

• • •

With Romeo and Juliet, you're talking about two people who
meet one night, and get married the same night. I believe in
love at first sight—but it hasn't happened to me yet.
—LEONARDO DiCAPRIO

• • •

I love him, and I don't care what you think. I love him for the
man he wants to be, and I love him for the man he almost is.
I love him.
—DOROTHY BOYD (RENEE ZELLWEGER), *Jerry Maguire*

• • •

The best smell in the world is that man that you love.
—JENNIFER ANISTON

• • •

We were convinced that there was no other life beneath the sky but ours. We believed that we would never die.
—DON JUAN (JOHNNY DEPP), *Don Juan DeMarco*

• • •

I want to tell you with my last breath that I have always loved you. I would rather be a ghost drifting by your side as a condemned soul than enter heaven without you. . . . Because of your love, I will never be a lonely spirit.
—LI MU BAI (CHOW YUN-FAT), *Crouching Tiger, Hidden Dragon*

• • •

When I am with you, my whole world is complete.
—ANONYMOUS

• • •

In many ways, unwise love is the truest love. Anyone can love a thing because. That's as easy as putting a penny in your pocket. But to love something despite. To know the flaws and love them too. That is rare and pure and perfect.
—PATRICK ROTHFUSS, *The Wise Man's Fear*

• • •

Each time you happen to me all over again.
—EDITH WHARTON, *The Age of Innocence*

• • •

I say if you love something, set it in a small cage and pester and smother it with love until it either loves you back or dies.
—MINDY KALING

• • •

I am going to fall in love with you. You don't have to love me back. I am going to give you my heart.
—CAROLINE (MARISA TOMEI), *Untamed Heart*

• • •

Don't say we are not right for each other. The way I see it is . . . we aren't right for anyone else.
—DOUG DORSEY (D. B. SWEENEY), *The Cutting Edge*

• • •

I would always rather be happy than dignified.
—CHARLOTTE BRONTË

• • •

CHAPTER 4

COMFORT

Each friend represents a world in us, a world possibly not born until they arrive, and it is only by this meeting that a new world is born.
—ANAÏS NIN

• • •

A friend is someone who knows all about you and still loves you.
—ELBERT HUBBARD

• • •

I think I fell in love with her a little bit. Isn't that dumb? But it was like I knew her. Like she was my oldest, dearest friend. The kind of person you can tell anything to, no matter how bad, and they'll still love you, because they know you.
—NEIL GAIMAN, *The Sandman Chronicles,*
Vol. 8: World's End

• • •

Happiness is only real when shared.
—JON KRAKAUER, *Into the Wild*

• • •

The man of knowledge must be able not only to love his enemies but also to hate his friends.
—FRIEDRICH NIETZSCHE

• • •

A friend is someone who gives you total freedom to be yourself—and especially to feel, or not to feel. Whatever you happen to be feeling at any moment is fine with them. That's what real love amounts to—letting a person be what he really is.
—JIM MORRISON

• • •

The ones that stay with you through everything—they're your true best friends. Don't let go of them.
—MARILYN MONROE

• • •

How many slams in an old screen door? Depends how loud you shut it. How many slices in a bread? Depends how thin you cut it. How much good inside a day? Depends how good you live 'em. How much love inside a friend? Depends how much you give 'em.
—SHEL SILVERSTEIN, *"How Many, How Much"*

• • •

To be brave is to love unconditionally without
expecting anything in return.
—MADONNA

• • •

Affection is responsible for nine-tenths of whatever solid and
durable happiness there is in our lives.
—C. S. LEWIS

• • •

We're born alone, we live alone, we die alone. Only through
our love and friendship can we create the illusion for the
moment that we're not alone.
—ORSON WELLES

• • •

The best thing to hold onto in life is each other.
—AUDREY HEPBURN

• • •

Once the realization is accepted that even between the closest
human beings infinite distances continue, a wonderful living
side by side can grow, if they succeed in loving the distance
between them which makes it possible for each to see the
other whole against the sky.
—RAINER MARIA RILKE

• • •

To be capable of steady friendship or lasting love, are the two
greatest proofs, not only of goodness of heart, but of strength
of mind.
—WILLIAM HAZLITT

• • •

The glory of friendship is not the outstretched hand, nor the kindly smile nor the joy of companionship; it is the spiritual inspiration that comes to one when he discovers that someone else believes in him and is willing to trust him.
—RALPH WALDO EMERSON

• • •

A real friend helps us think our best thoughts, do our noblest deeds, be our finest selves.
—ANONYMOUS

• • •

If a man does not make new acquaintance as he advances through life, he will soon find himself left alone. A man, Sir, should keep his friendship in constant repair.
—SAMUEL JOHNSON

• • •

The friendships of the world are oft confederacies in vice, or leagues of pleasure; ours has severest virtue for its basis, and such a friendship ends not but with life.
—JOSEPH ADDISON, *Cato, a Tragedy*

• • •

He who has a thousand friends has not a friend to spare, and he who has one enemy will meet him everywhere.
—ALI, *A Hundred Sayings*

• • •

Love is only chatter, friends are all that matter.
—GELETT BURGESS, *A Gage of Youth: Lyrics from The Lark and Other Poems*

• • •

Fate chooses our relatives, we choose our friends.
—JACQUES DELILLE, *Malheur et Pitié*

• • •

The only way to have a friend is to be one.
—RALPH WALDO EMERSON, *Essays*

• • •

A friendship that can be ended didn't ever start.
—MELLIN DE SAINT-GELAIS, *Oeuvres Poétiques*

• • •

Of two friends, one is always the slave of the other, although frequently neither acknowledges the fact to himself.
—MIKHAIL LERMONTOV, *A Hero of Our Time*

• • •

Can miles truly separate you from friends? . . . If you want to be with someone you love, aren't you already there?
—RICHARD BACH

• • •

A more appropriate adjective for measuring the degree of a friendship should be "good"—how good rather than "close"—how close. A good friend is not necessarily close; a close friend is not necessarily good.
—JOHN NEWTON, PhD, *Complete Conduct Principles for the 21st Century*

• • •

Friendship is Love without his wings!
—GEORGE GORDON BYRON, "L'Amitié est l'Amour
sans Ailes"

• • •

The better part of one's life consists of his friendships.
—ABRAHAM LINCOLN, *Letter to Joseph Gillespie*

• • •

To desire the same things and to reject the same things
constitutes true friendship.
—SALLUST, *The Conspiracy of Catiline*

• • •

Friendship is a cadence of divine melody melting
through the heart.
—CHARLES MILDWAY

• • •

Remember, George: no man is a failure who has friends.
—CLARENCE (HENRY TRAVERS), *It's a Wonderful Life*

• • •

I never had any friends later on like the ones I had when
I was twelve.
—THE WRITER (RICHARD DREYFUSS), *Stand by Me*

• • •

Let the rest of the world beat their brains out for a buck.
It's friends that count. And I got friends.
—MAX FABIAN (GREGORY RATOFF), *All About Eve*

• • •

You are my superior officer. You are also my friend. I have
been and always shall be yours.
—SPOCK (LEONARD NIMOY), *Star Trek II:*
The Wrath of Khan

• • •

I have a dream too, but it's about singing and dancing and
making people happy. It's the kind of dream that gets better
the more people you share it with. And I found a whole
group of friends who have the same dream, and that makes
us sort of like a family.
—KERMIT THE FROG, *The Muppet Movie*

• • •

Oh, you're the best friends anybody ever had. And it's
funny, but I feel as if I'd known you all the time, but I couldn't
have, could I?
—DOROTHY (JUDY GARLAND), *The Wizard of Oz*

• • •

It's an insane world, but in it there is one sanity;
the loyalty of old friends.
—MESSALA (STEPHEN BOYD), *Ben-Hur*

• • •

It is the friends that you can call at 4 a.m. that matter.
—MARLENE DIETRICH

• • •

Hold a true friend with both your hands.
—NIGERIAN PROVERB

• • •

You drew me from the darkest period of my young life,
sharing with me the sacred mystery of what it is to be an
artist. I learned to see through you and never compose a
line or draw a curve that does not come from the knowledge
I derived in our precious time together.
—PATTI SMITH, *Just Kids*

• • •

It's bullshit to think of friendship and romance as being
different. They're not. They're just variations of the same love.
Variations of the same desire to be close.
—RACHEL COHN, *Naomi and Eli's No Kiss List*

• • •

If you remember me, then I don't care if everyone else forgets.
—HARUKI MURAKAMI, *Kafka on the Shore*

• • •

It is a curious thought, but it is only when you see people
looking ridiculous that you realize just how much
you love them.
—AGATHA CHRISTIE, *An Autobiography*

• • •

Mothers are endowed with a love that is unlike any
other love on the face of the earth.
—MARJORIE PAY HINCKLEY

• • •

There is nothing I would not do for those who are really my
friends. I have no notion of loving people by halves, it is not
my nature.
—JANE AUSTEN, *Northanger Abbey*

• • •

I think it's important to make time for the people in your life
who you love and who love you back.
—KEIRA KNIGHTLEY

• • •

The gifts of an honorable, well-lived life are in those who will
miss you once you're gone.
—DON WILLIAMS JR.

• • •

Choose people who will lift you up. Find people who will
make you better.
—MICHELLE OBAMA

• • •

An acquaintance merely enjoys your company, a fair-weather companion flatters when all is well, a true friend has your best interests at heart and the pluck to tell you what you need to hear.
—E. A. BUCCHIANERI, *Brushstrokes of a Gadfly*

• • •

The capacity for friendship is God's way of apologizing for our families.
—JAY McINERNEY, *The Last of the Savages*

• • •

You must remember, family is often born of blood, but it doesn't depend on blood. Nor is it exclusive of friendship. Family members can be your best friends, you know. And best friends, whether or not they are related to you, can be your family.
—TRENTON LEE STEWART,
The Mysterious Benedict Society

• • •

I sustain myself with the love of family.
—MAYA ANGELOU

• • •

Home is where you are loved the most and act the worst.
—MARJORIE PAY HINCKLEY

• • •

Friends are part of the glue that holds life and faith
together. Powerful stuff.
—JON KATZ

• • •

One friend with whom you have a lot in common is
better than three with whom you struggle to find things
to talk about. We never needed best friend gear because
I guess with real friends you don't have to make it official.
It just is.
—MINDY KALING, *Is Everyone Hanging Out Without Me?*

• • •

CHAPTER 5

WISDOM

If you judge people, you have no time to love them.
—MOTHER TERESA

• • •

The only thing we never get enough of is love; and the only
thing we never give enough of is love.
—HENRY MILLER

• • •

Do not pity the dead, Harry. Pity the living, and, above all
those who live without love.
—J. K. ROWLING, *Harry Potter and the Deathly Hallows*

• • •

And now these three remain: faith, hope, and love. But the
greatest of these is love.
—CORINTHIANS 13:13

• • •

We waste time looking for the perfect lover, instead of
creating the perfect love.
—TOM ROBBINS

• • •

The art of love is largely the art of persistence.
—ALBERT ELLIS

• • •

All love shifts and changes. I don't know if you can be
wholeheartedly in love all the time.
—JULIE ANDREWS

• • •

Lost love is still love. It takes a different form, that's all. You can't see their smile or bring them food or tousle their hair or move them around a dance floor. But when those senses weaken another heightens. Memory. Memory becomes your partner. You nurture it. You hold it. You dance with it.
—MITCH ALBOM

• • •

What is hell? I maintain that it is the suffering of being unable to love.
—FYODOR DOSTOYEVSKY, *The Brothers Karamazov*

• • •

I do not trust people who don't love themselves and yet tell me, "I love you." There is an African saying which is: be careful when a naked person offers you a shirt.
—MAYA ANGELOU

• • •

When you trip over love, it is easy to get up. But when you fall
in love, it is impossible to stand again.
—ALBERT EINSTEIN

• • •

If a thing loves, it is infinite.
The great tragedy of life is not that men perish, but that they
cease to love.
—W. SOMERSET MAUGHAM

• • •

If someone thinks that peace and love are just a cliché that
must have been left behind in the Sixties, that's a problem.
Peace and love are eternal.
—JOHN LENNON

• • •

The heart is a museum, filled with the exhibits of a lifetime's loves.
—DIANE ACKERMAN

• • •

People should fall in love with their eyes closed.
—ANDY WARHOL

• • •

We can only learn to love by loving.
—IRIS MURDOCH

• • •

When we are in love, we seem to ourselves quite different from what we were before.
—BLAISE PASCAL

• • •

To fear love is to fear life, and those who fear life are already
three-parts dead.
—BERTRAND RUSSELL

• • •

It doesn't matter who you are or what you look like, so long as
somebody loves you.
—ROALD DAHL, *The Witches*

• • •

Where there is great love, there are always miracles.
—WILLA CATHER

• • •

Remember that the best relationship is one in which your love
for each other exceeds your need for each other.
—DALAI LAMA XIV

• • •

True love is the best thing in the world, except for cough
drops.
—WILLIAM GOLDMAN, *The Princess Bride*

• • •

There is only one happiness in life—to love and to be loved.
—GEORGE SAND

• • •

A simple "I love you" means more than money.
—FRANK SINATRA

• • •

Sometimes the heart sees what is invisible to the eye.
—H. JACKSON BROWN JR.

• • •

Sexiness is a state of mind—a comfortable state of being. It's about loving yourself in your most unlovable moments.
—HALLE BERRY

• • •

You don't marry one person; you marry three: the person you think they are, the person they are, and the person they are going to become as the result of being.
—RICHARD J. NEEDHAM

• • •

Love is like a friendship caught on fire. In the beginning a flame, very pretty, often hot and fierce, but still only light and flickering. As love grows older, our hearts mature and our love becomes as coals, deep-burning and unquenchable.
—BRUCE LEE

• • •

Let us always meet each other with a smile, for the smile is the beginning of love.
—MOTHER TERESA

• • •

A man reserves his true and deepest love not for the species of woman in whose company he finds himself electrified and enkindled, but for that one in whose company he may feel tenderly drowsy.
—GEORGE JEAN NATHAN

• • •

A flower cannot blossom without sunshine, and man cannot live without love.
—MAX MULLER

• • •

A kiss is a lovely trick designed by nature to stop speech when words become superfluous.
—INGRID BERGMAN

• • •

Love yourself first and everything else falls into line.
You really have to love yourself to get anything done
in this world.
—LUCILLE BALL

• • •

Love is a better teacher than duty.
—ALBERT EINSTEIN

• • •

We love life, not because we are used to living but because we
are used to loving.
—FRIEDRICH NIETZSCHE

• • •

We don't love to be loved; we love to love.
—LEO BUSCAGLIA

• • •

What we have once enjoyed we can never lose. All that we
love deeply becomes a part of us.
—HELEN KELLER

• • •

Love isn't something you find. Love is something that
finds you.
—LORETTA YOUNG

• • •

Life without love is like a tree without blossoms or fruit.
—KHALIL GIBRAN, *The Prophet*

• • •

Faith makes all things possible . . . love makes all things easy.
—DWIGHT L. MOODY

• • •

A kiss makes the heart young again and wipes out the years.
—RUPERT BROOKE

• • •

The best proof of love is trust.
—JOYCE BROTHERS

• • •

A very small degree of hope is sufficient to cause the
birth of love.
—STENDHAL

• • •

Love makes your soul crawl out from its hiding place.
—ZORA NEALE HURSTON

• • •

A pair of powerful spectacles has sometimes sufficed to
cure a person in love.
—FRIEDRICH NIETZSCHE

• • •

The giving of love is an education in itself.
—ELEANOR ROOSEVELT

• • •

All mankind love a lover.
—RALPH WALDO EMERSON, *Essays: First Series*

• • •

For small creatures such as we the vastness is bearable only
through love.
—CARL SAGAN, *Contact*

• • •

If you would be loved, love and be lovable.
—BENJAMIN FRANKLIN, *Poor Richard's Almanac*

• • •

Everybody needs love. There are a lot of guys that you think
are hard-core gangsters, but all these guys' weaknesses are
women. Look at the movie *Scarface.* At the end of the day,
all he wanted to do was to have kids with his woman.
—MASTER P

• • •

There's no bad consequence to loving fully, with all your heart. You always gain by giving love. It's like that beautiful Shakespeare quote from *Romeo and Juliet*: "My bounty is as boundless as the sea. My love is deep. The more I give to thee, the more I have. For both are infinite."
—REESE WITHERSPOON

• • •

Let no one who loves be called altogether unhappy. Even love unreturned has its rainbow.
—J. M. BARRIE, *The Little Minister*

• • •

It is sad not to be loved, but it is much sadder not to be able to love.
—MIGUEL DE UNAMUNO, *To a Young Writer*

• • •

Only do what your heart tells you.
—PRINCESS DIANA

• • •

Anyone who falls in love is searching for the missing pieces of themselves. So anyone who's in love gets sad when they think of their lover. It's like stepping back inside a room you have fond memories of, one you haven't seen in a long time.
—HARUKI MURAKAMI

• • •

I refuse to let what happened to me make me bitter. I still completely believe in love and I'm open to anything that will happen to me.
—NICOLE KIDMAN

• • •

My great hope is to laugh as much as I cry; to get my work
done and try to love somebody and have the courage to accept
the love in return.
—MAYA ANGELOU

• • •

Love involves a peculiar unfathomable combination of
understanding and misunderstanding.
—DIANE ARBUS

• • •

Painting is like making love. You cannot ask, "How do you do
it?" But, hopefully, it is beautiful.
—FRANCESCO CLEMENTE

• • •

Love much. Earth has enough of bitter in it.
—ELLA WHEELER WILCOX

• • •

The supreme happiness of life is the conviction that
we are loved.
—VICTOR HUGO

• • •

We are told that people stay in love because of chemistry, or
because they remain intrigued with each other, because of
many kindnesses, because of luck. But part of it has got to be
forgiveness and gratefulness.
—ELLEN GOODMAN

• • •

Even when love isn't enough . . . somehow it is.
—STEPHEN KING

• • •

If you have only one smile in you, give it to the people
you love.
—MAYA ANGELOU

• • •

The only creatures that are evolved enough to convey pure
love are dogs and infants.
—JOHNNY DEPP

• • •

There's no substitute for a great love who says, "No matter what's wrong with you, you're welcome at this table."
—TOM HANKS

• • •

Passion makes the world go round. Love just makes it a safer place.
—ICE T

• • •

Everything is clearer when you're in love.
—JOHN LENNON

• • •

True love cannot be found where it does not truly exist;
nor can it be hidden where it does.
—DAVID SCHWIMMER

• • •

There is a place you can touch a woman that will drive her
crazy. Her heart.
—MELANIE GRIFFITH

• • •

You can't put a price tag on love, but you can on all its
accessories.
—MELANIE CLARK

• • •

Love doesn't want people to stay ignorant and frightened. Love doesn't value obedience over all else. Love doesn't judge and find some lives—or loves—more valuable than others. Love doesn't use people and throw them away. Love stays, and makes you stronger, even when the person you love is gone.
—STACEY JAY, *Juliet Immortal*

• • •

A person who loves is a righteous person, and if someone has the ability and desire to show love to another—to someone willing to receive it, then for goodness' sake, let them do it.
—FIONA APPLE, *Letter to Bill Magee*

• • •

A person who exists only for the sake of his loved one is not an independent entity, but a spiritual parasite. The love of a parasite is worth nothing.
—AYN RAND, *Little Big Book of Life*

• • •

If there's a thing I've learned in my life it's to not be afraid of the responsibility that comes with caring for other people. What we do for love: those things endure. Even if the people you do them for don't.
—CASSANDRA CLARE

• • •

When you love someone you let them take care of you.
—JODI PICOULT

• • •

The fate of your heart is your choice and no one else gets a vote.
—SARAH DESSEN, *This Lullaby*

• • •

Love itself is what is left over when being in love has burned
away, and this is both an art and a fortunate accident.
—LOUIS DE BERNIÈRES, *Captain Corelli's Mandolin*

• • •

Hate the sin, love the sinner.
—MAHATMA GANDHI

• • •

You can't measure the mutual affection of two human beings
by the number of words they exchange.
—MILAN KUNDERA, *Identity*

• • •

Love hard when there is love to be had. Because perfect guys don't exist, but there's always one guy that is perfect for you.
—BOB MARLEY

• • •

There are two basic motivating forces: fear and love. When we are afraid, we pull back from life. When we are in love, we open to all that life has to offer with passion, excitement, and acceptance. We need to learn to love ourselves first, in all our glory and our imperfections. If we cannot love ourselves, we cannot fully open to our ability to love others or our potential to create. Evolution and all hopes for a better world rest in the fearlessness and open-hearted vision of people who embrace life.
—JOHN LENNON

• • •

A book without words is like love without a kiss; it's empty.
—ANDREW WOLFE

• • •

I am certainly not an authority on love because there are no authorities on love, just those who've had luck with it and those who haven't.
—BILL COSBY

• • •

Without love in your life, you have nothing.
—WYNONNA JUDD

• • •

I've always said that I expected to grow up and get married like any nice southern girl, but the fact is you don't get married in the abstract. You find someone that you'd like to be married to.
—CONDOLEEZZA RICE

• • •

I try to believe like I believed when I was five . . . when your
heart tells you everything you need to know.
—LUCY LIU

• • •

That's what people do who love you. They put their arms
around you and love you when you're not so lovable.
—DEB CALETTI

• • •

Choose love over fear.
—OPRAH WINFREY

• • •

My number one rule for romance is surprise.
—HUGH JACKMAN

• • •

If you're a woman and a guy's ever said anything romantic
to you, he just left off the second part that would have made
you sick if you could have heard it.
—LOUIS C. K.

• • •

If you can love your enemy, you already have victory.
—PREACHER GREEN (DAVID OYELOWO), *The Help*

• • •

Love doesn't just sit there, like a stone, it has to be made,
like bread; remade all the time, made new.
—URSULA K. LE GUIN

• • •

CHAPTER 6

POWER

Take away love and our earth is a tomb.
—ROBERT BROWNING

• • •

You are protected, in short, by your ability to love.
—J. K. ROWLING, *Harry Potter and the Half-Blood Prince*

• • •

Darkness cannot drive out darkness: only light can do that.
Hate cannot drive out hate: only love can do that.
—MARTIN LUTHER KING JR., *A Testament of Hope:*
The Essential Writings and Speeches

• • •

Being deeply loved by someone gives you strength, while
loving someone deeply gives you courage.
—LAO TZU

• • •

I am nothing special, of this I am sure. I am a common man
with common thoughts and I've led a common life. There are
no monuments dedicated to me and my name will soon be
forgotten, but I've loved another with all my heart and soul,
and to me, this has always been enough.
—NICHOLAS SPARKS, *The Notebook*

• • •

Every heart sings a song, incomplete, until another heart
whispers back. Those who wish to sing always find a song.
At the touch of a lover, everyone becomes a poet.
—PLATO

• • •

There's nothing you can ever do to lose my love. I will protect
you until you die, and after your death I will still protect
you. I am stronger than Depression and I am braver than
Loneliness and nothing will ever exhaust me.
—ELIZABETH GILBERT, *Eat, Pray, Love*

• • •

The world is indeed full of peril and in it there are many
dark places. But still there is much that is fair. And though
in all lands, love is now mingled with grief, it still grows,
perhaps, the greater.
—J. R. R. TOLKIEN, *The Lord of the Rings*

• • •

I fell in love with her courage, her sincerity, and her flaming self-respect. And it's these things I'd believe in, even if the whole world indulged in wild suspicions that she wasn't all she should be. I love her and it is the beginning of everything.
—F. SCOTT FITZGERALD

• • •

It is good to love many things, for therein lies the true strength, and whosoever loves much performs much, and can accomplish much, and what is done in love is well done.
—VINCENT VAN GOGH

• • •

Love recognizes no barriers. It jumps hurdles, leaps fences, penetrates walls to arrive at its destination full of hope.
—MAYA ANGELOU

• • •

Even after all this time, the sun never says to the earth,
"You owe me." Look what happens with a love like that.
It lights up the whole sky.
—HAFIZ

• • •

High thanks I owe you, excellent lovers, who carry out the
world for me to new and noble depths, and enlarge the
meaning of all my thoughts.
—RALPH WALDO EMERSON, *Essays: First Series*

• • •

The moment you have in your heart this extraordinary thing
called love and feel the depth, the delight, the ecstasy of it,
you will discover that for you the world is transformed.
—JIDDU KRISHNAMURTI

• • •

Someday, after mastering the winds, the waves, the tides and gravity, we shall harness for God the energies of love, and then, for a second time in the history of the world, man will have discovered fire.
—PIERRE TEILHARD DE CHARDIN

• • •

Death cannot stop true love. All it can do is delay it for a while.
—WILLIAM GOLDMAN, *The Princess Bride*

• • •

It is love, not reason, that is stronger than death.
—THOMAS MANN

• • •

What's the earth with all its art, verse, music, worth—
compared with love, found, gained, and kept?
—ROBERT BROWNING

• • •

Everything that I understand, I understand only because
I love.
—LEO TOLSTOY

• • •

In true love it is the soul that envelops the body.
—FRIEDRICH NIETZSCHE

• • •

Till I loved I never lived—enough.
—EMILY DICKINSON

• • •

For someone like me who is obsessed with organization and planning, I love the idea that love is the one exception to that. Love is the one wild card.
—TAYLOR SWIFT

• • •

For chances are that at some point along the line you will hold in your hands another person's heart. There is no greater responsibility on the planet. However you contend with this fragile organ, which pounds or seizes in accordance with your caprice, will take your full measure.
—LIONEL SHRIVER, *The Post-Birthday World*

• • •

I think it is all a matter of love; the more you love a memory
the stronger and stranger it becomes.
—VLADIMIR NABOKOV

• • •

"And what would humans be without love?"
Rare, said Death.
—TERRY PRATCHETT, *Sourcery*

• • •

When I say it's you I like, I'm talking about that part of you
that knows that life is far more than anything you can ever
see or hear or touch. That deep part of you that allows you
to stand for those things without which humankind cannot
survive. Love that conquers hate, peace that rises triumphant
over war, and justice that proves more powerful than greed.
—FRED ROGERS

• • •

I realized: love won't obey our expectations. Its mystery is pure and absolute.
—FRANCESCA JOHNSON (MERYL STREEP), *The Bridges of Madison County*

• • •

I know a lot about love. I've seen it, centuries and centuries of it, and it was the only thing that made watching your world bearable. All those wars. Pain and lies, hate . . . It made me want to turn away and never look down again. But to see the way that mankind loves . . . You could search to the furthest reaches of the universe and never find anything more beautiful.
—YVAINE (CLAIRE DANES), *Stardust*

Index